This Belongs To:

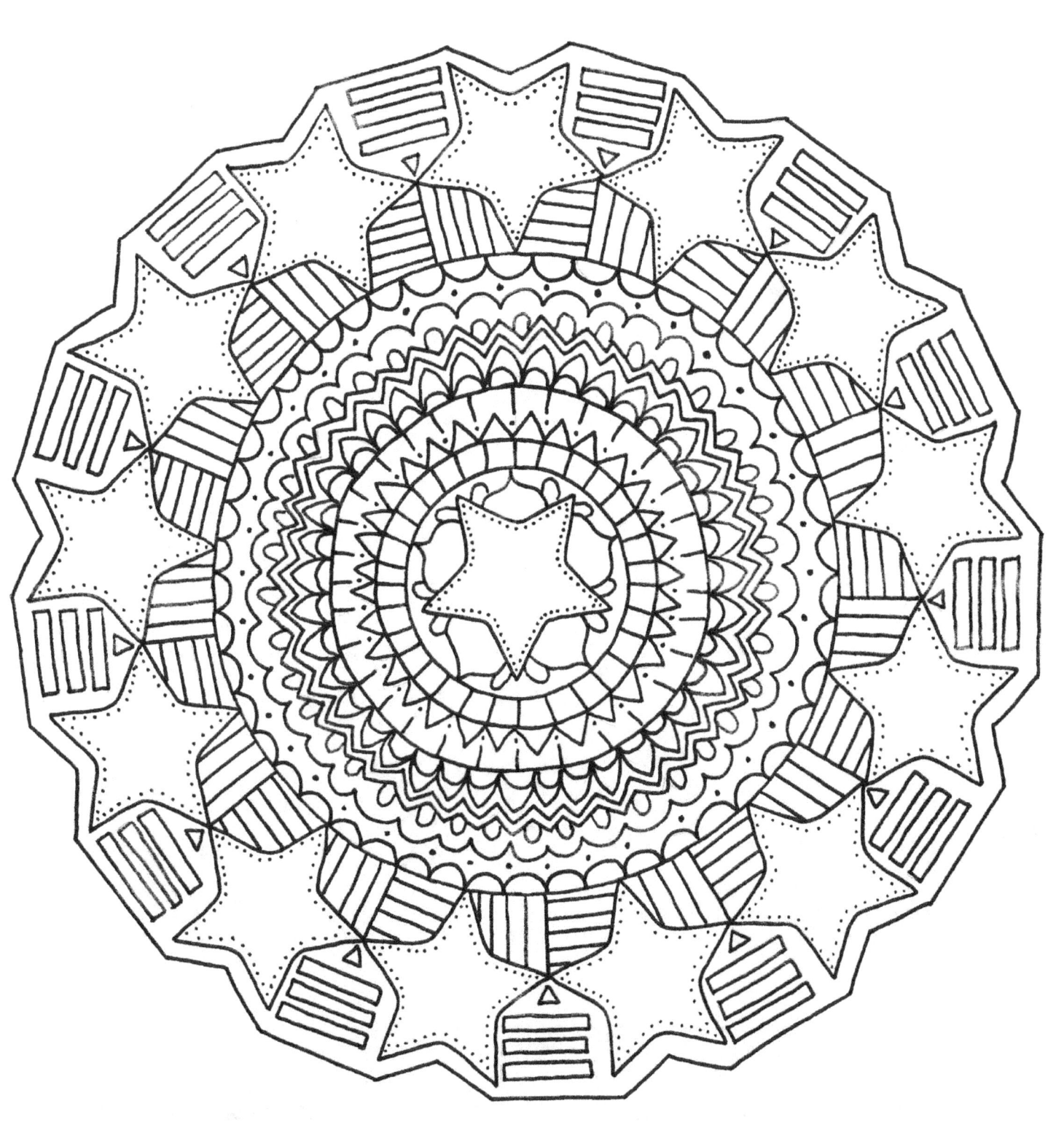

"The sun has one kind of splendor, the moon another and the stars another; and the star differs from star in splendor."
1 Corinthians 15:41

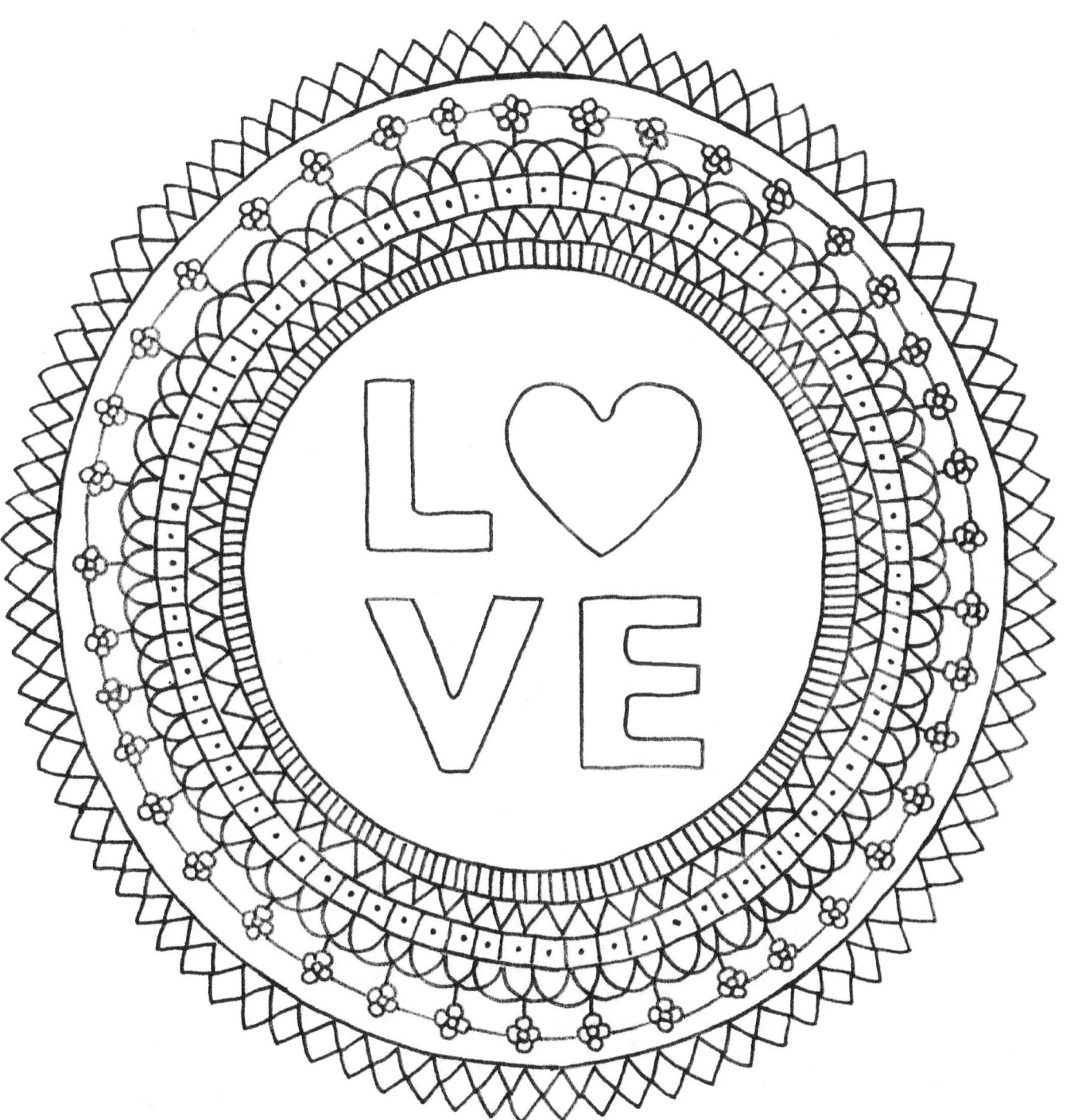

"Do everything in love."

1 Corinthians 16:14

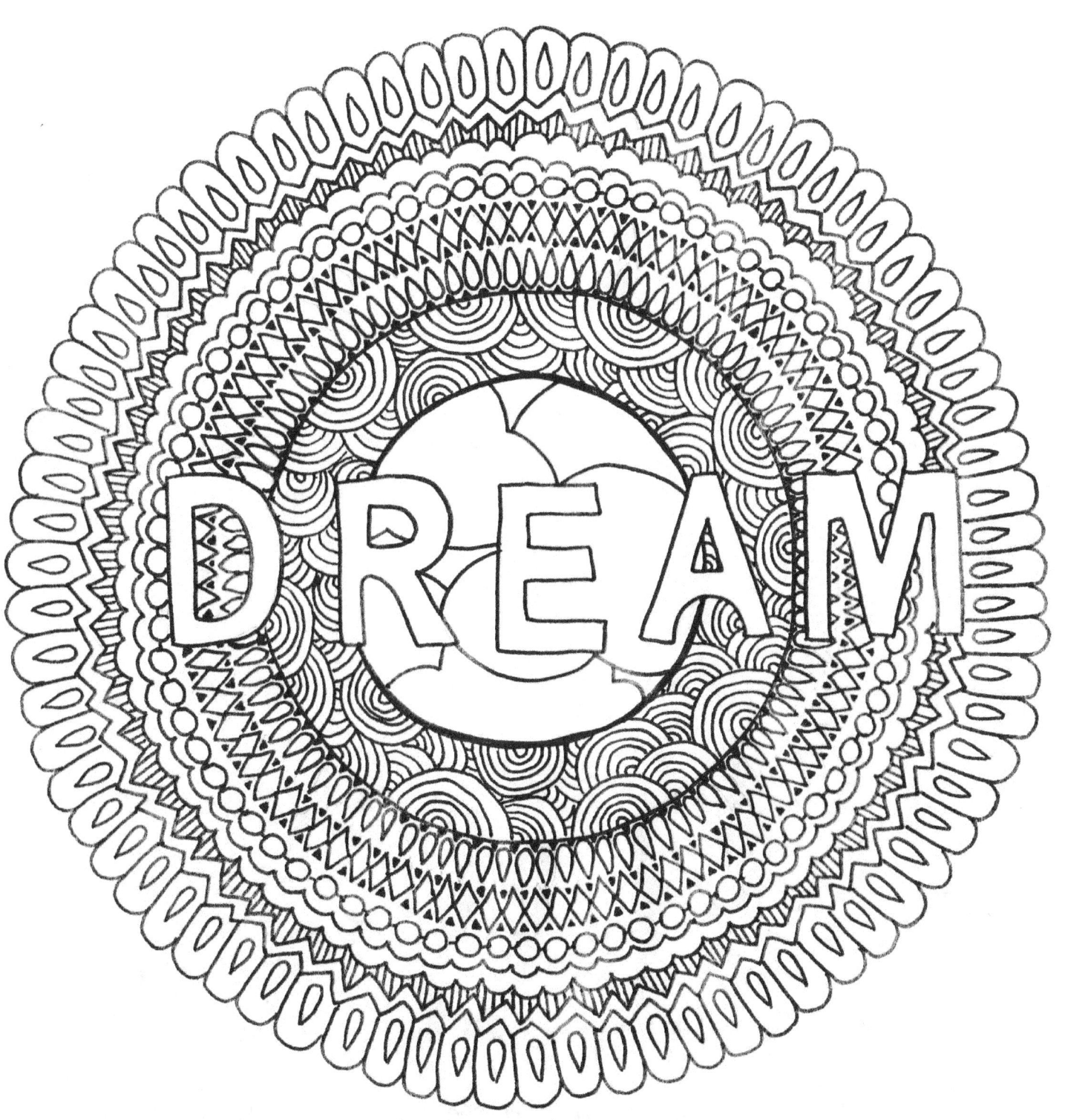

"For God does speak - now one way, now another - though no one perceives it."
Job 33:14

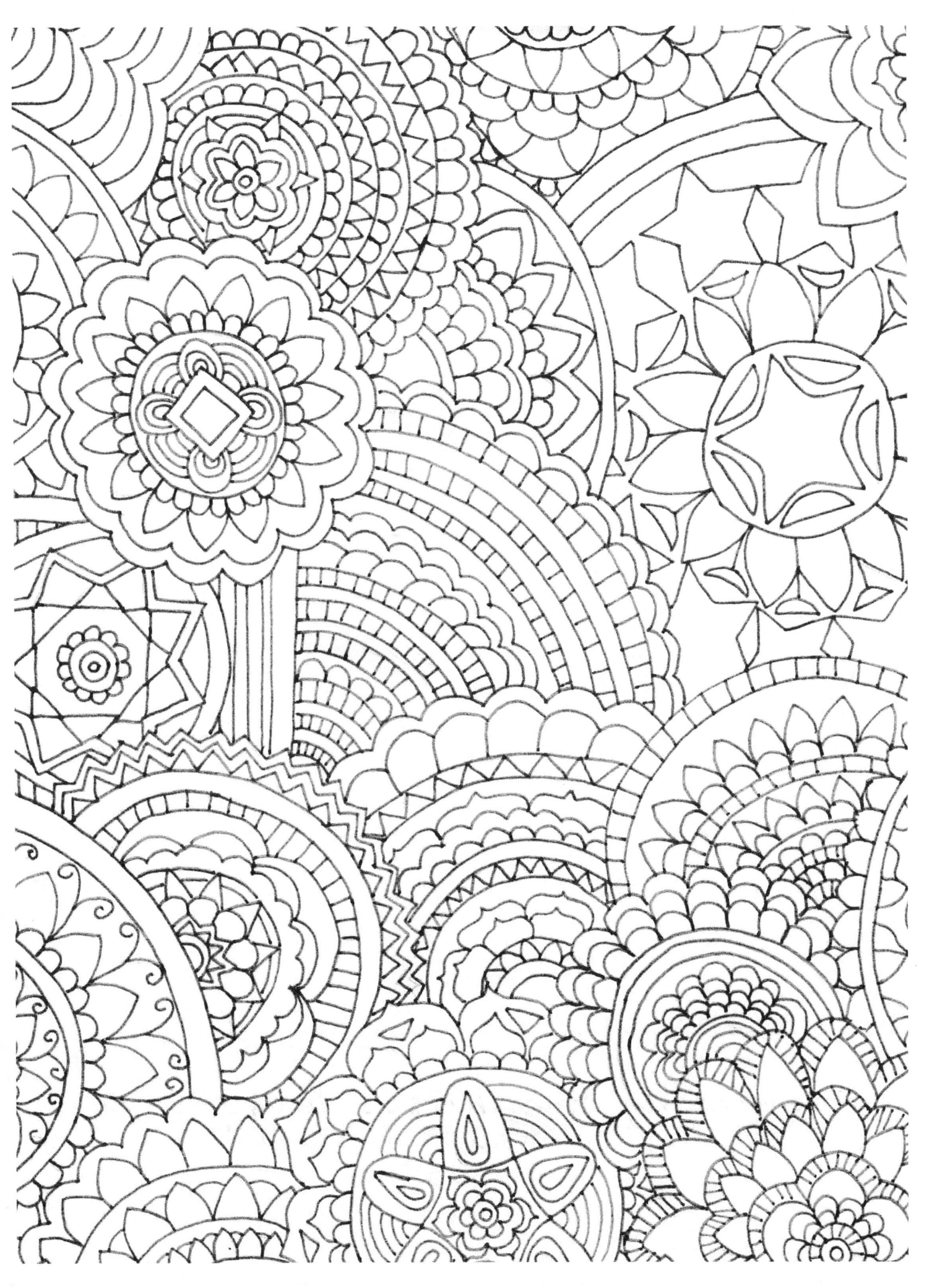

"Overhearing what they said, Jesus told him,
'Don't be afraid; just believe.'"
Mark 5:36

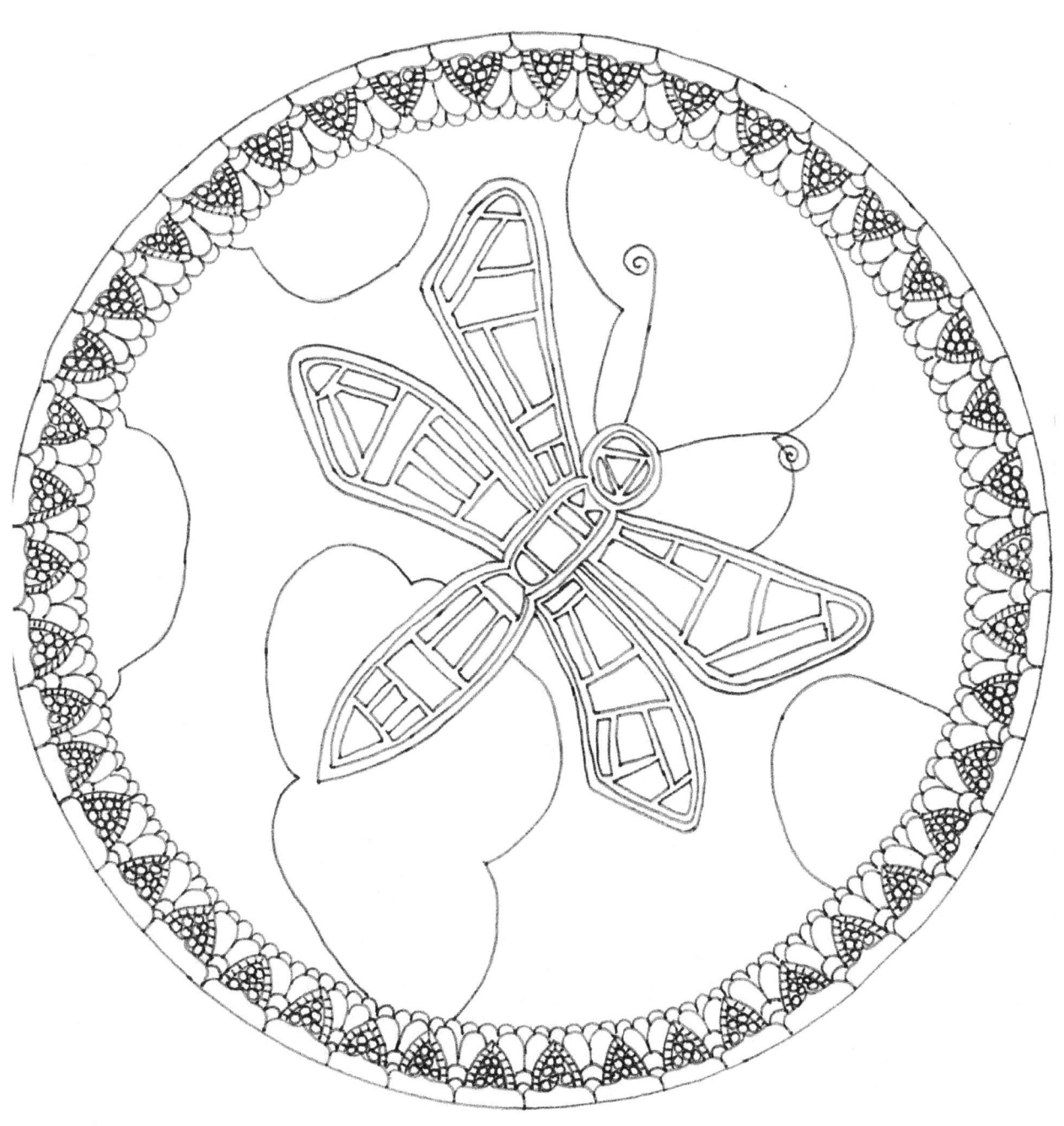

"Do not grieve, for the joy of the Lord is your strenght,"
Nehemiah 8:10

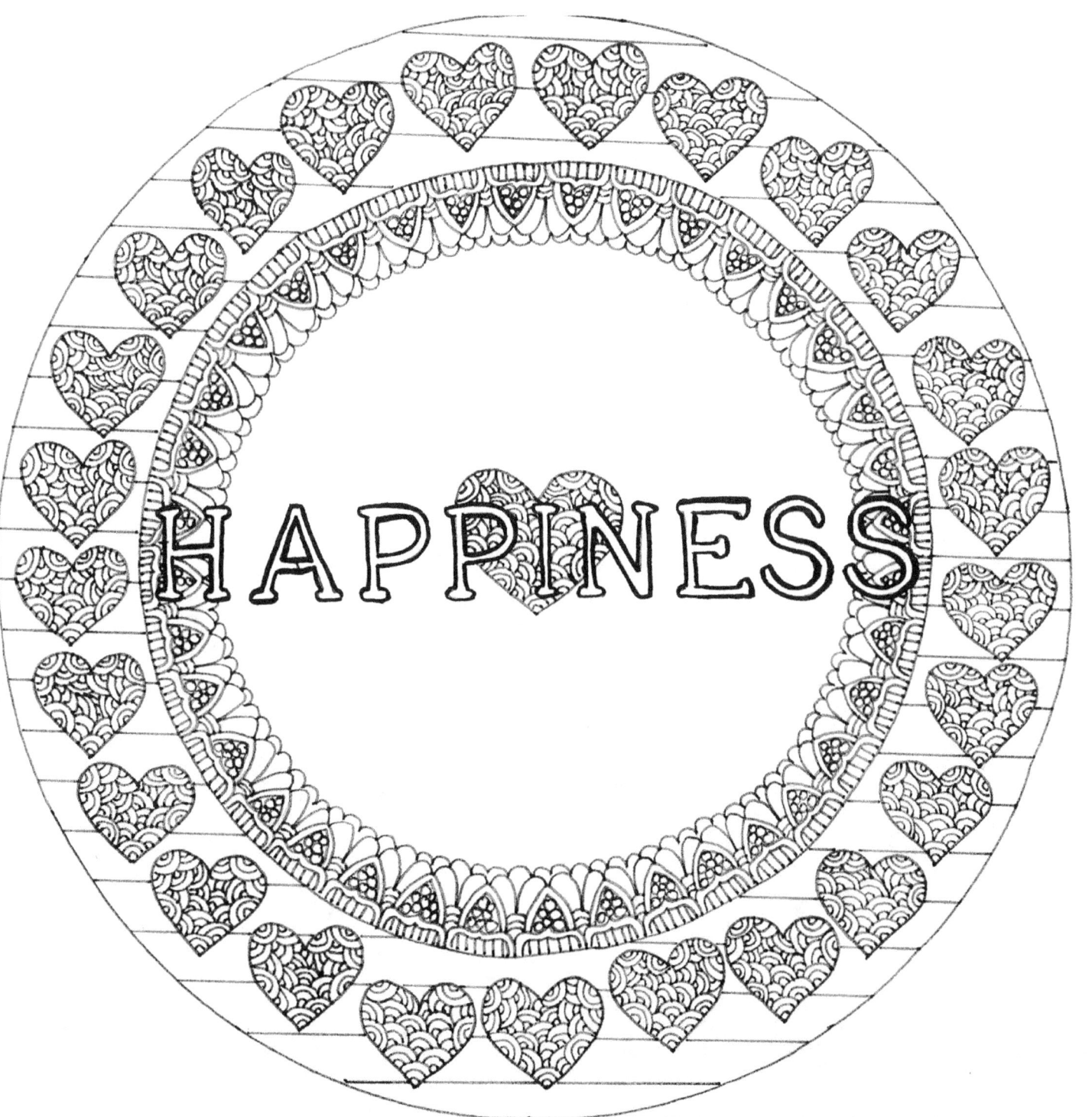

"Those who plant in tears will harvest with shouts of joy."
Psalm 126:5

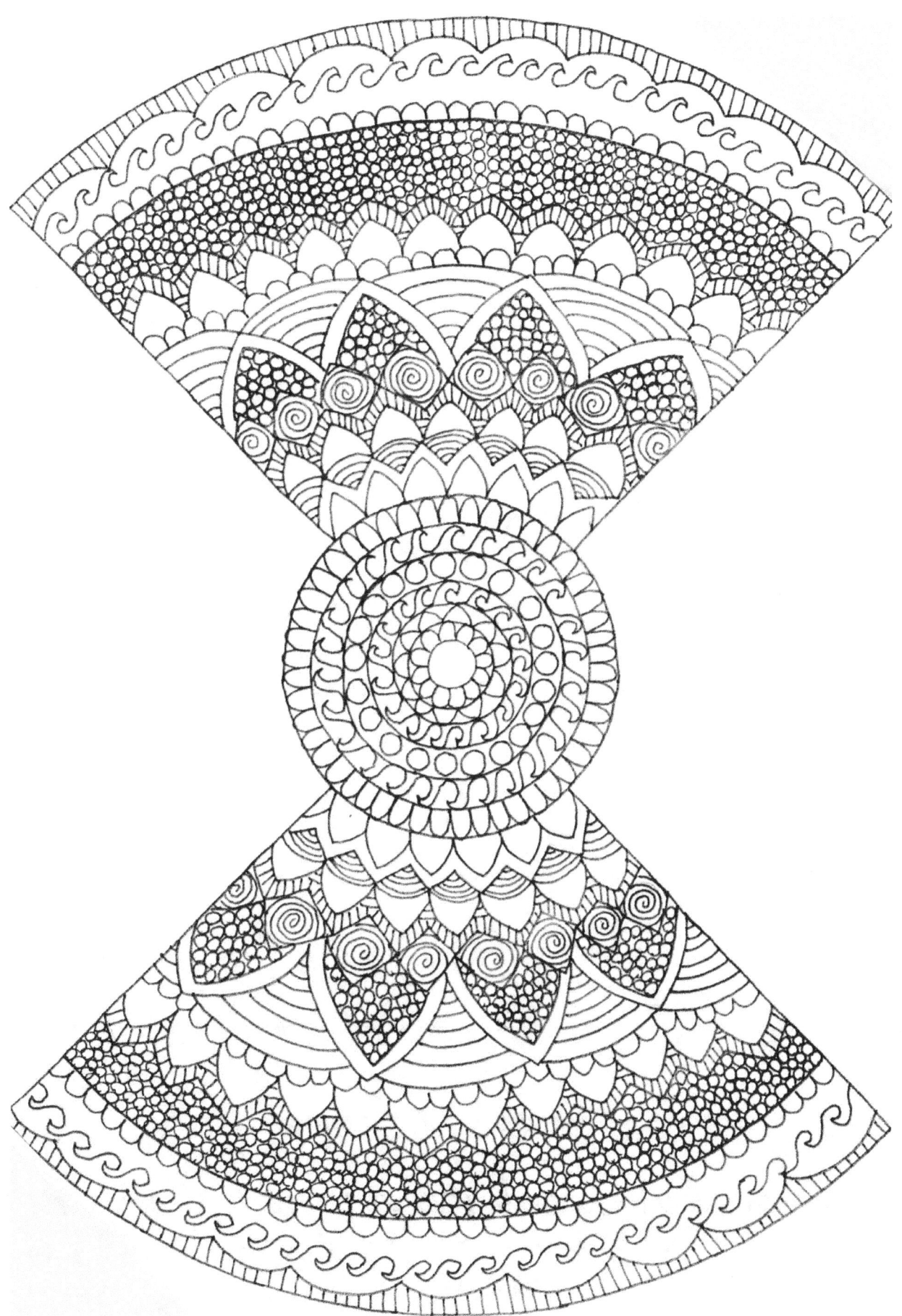

"Be on your guard; stand firm in the faith;
be courageous; be strong."
1 Corinthians 16:13

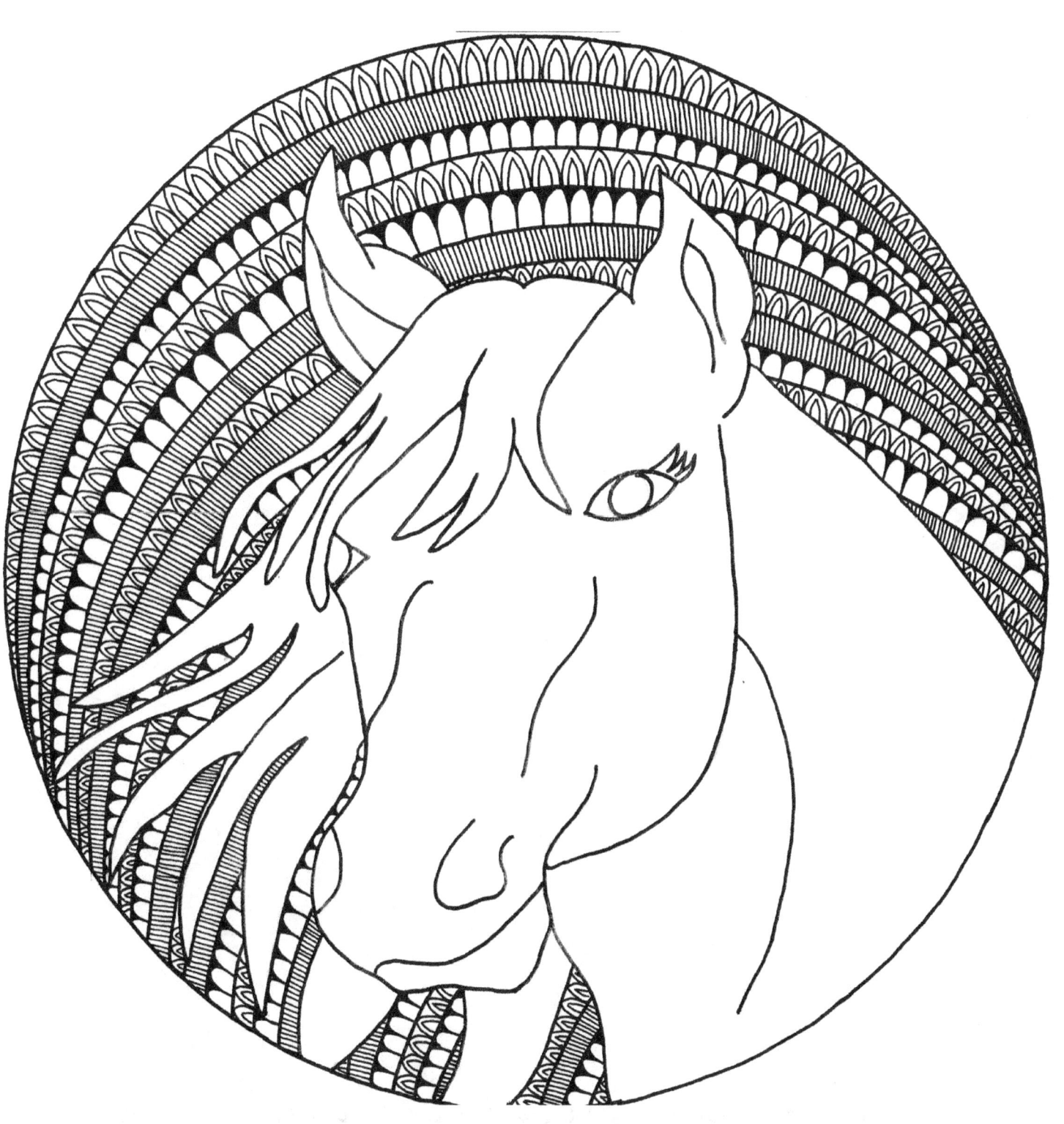

"Watch the path of your feet And all your ways will be established."
Proverbs 4:26

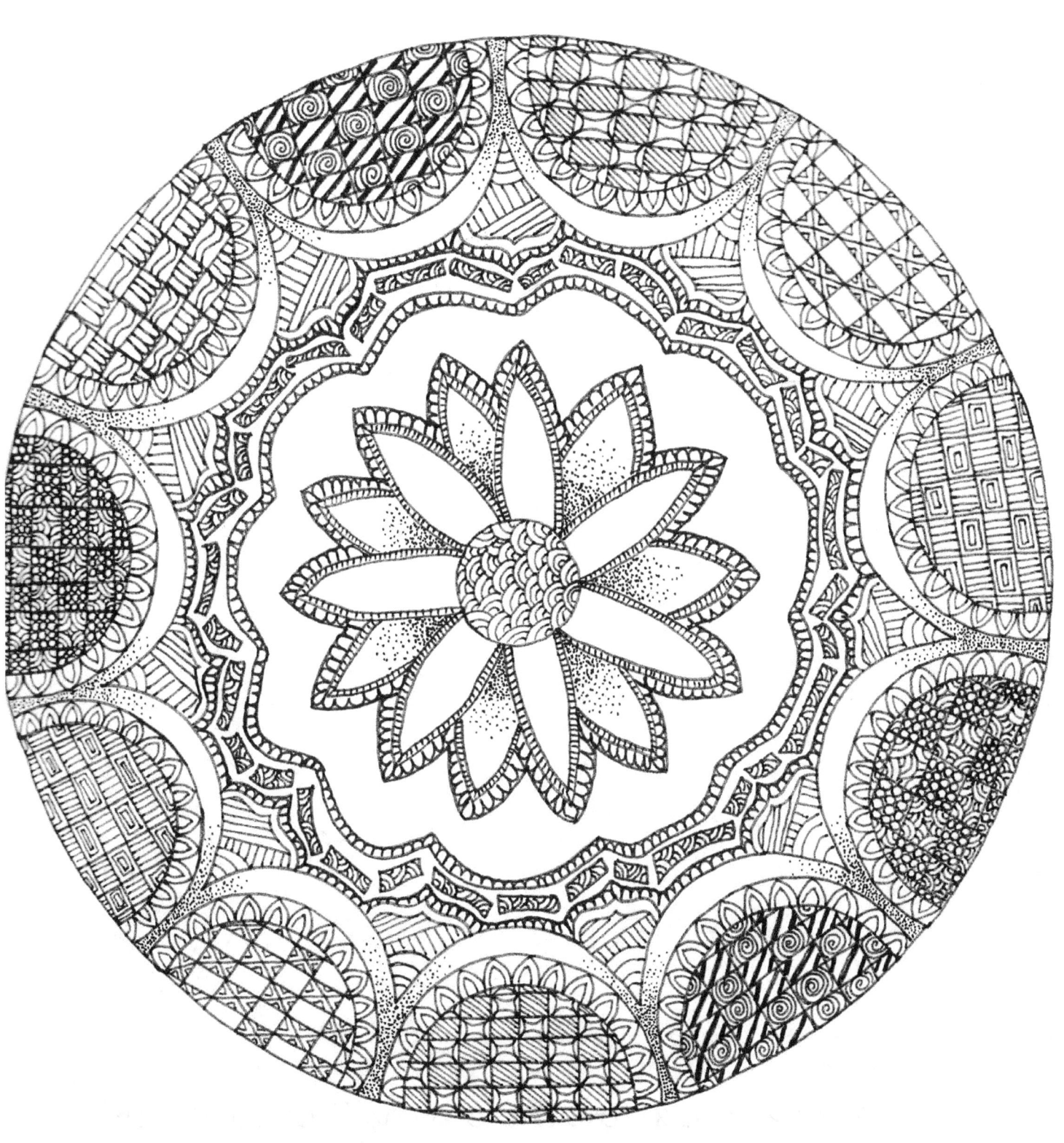

"Flowers appear on the earth; the season of singing has come, the cooing of doves is heard in our land."
Song of Songs 2:12

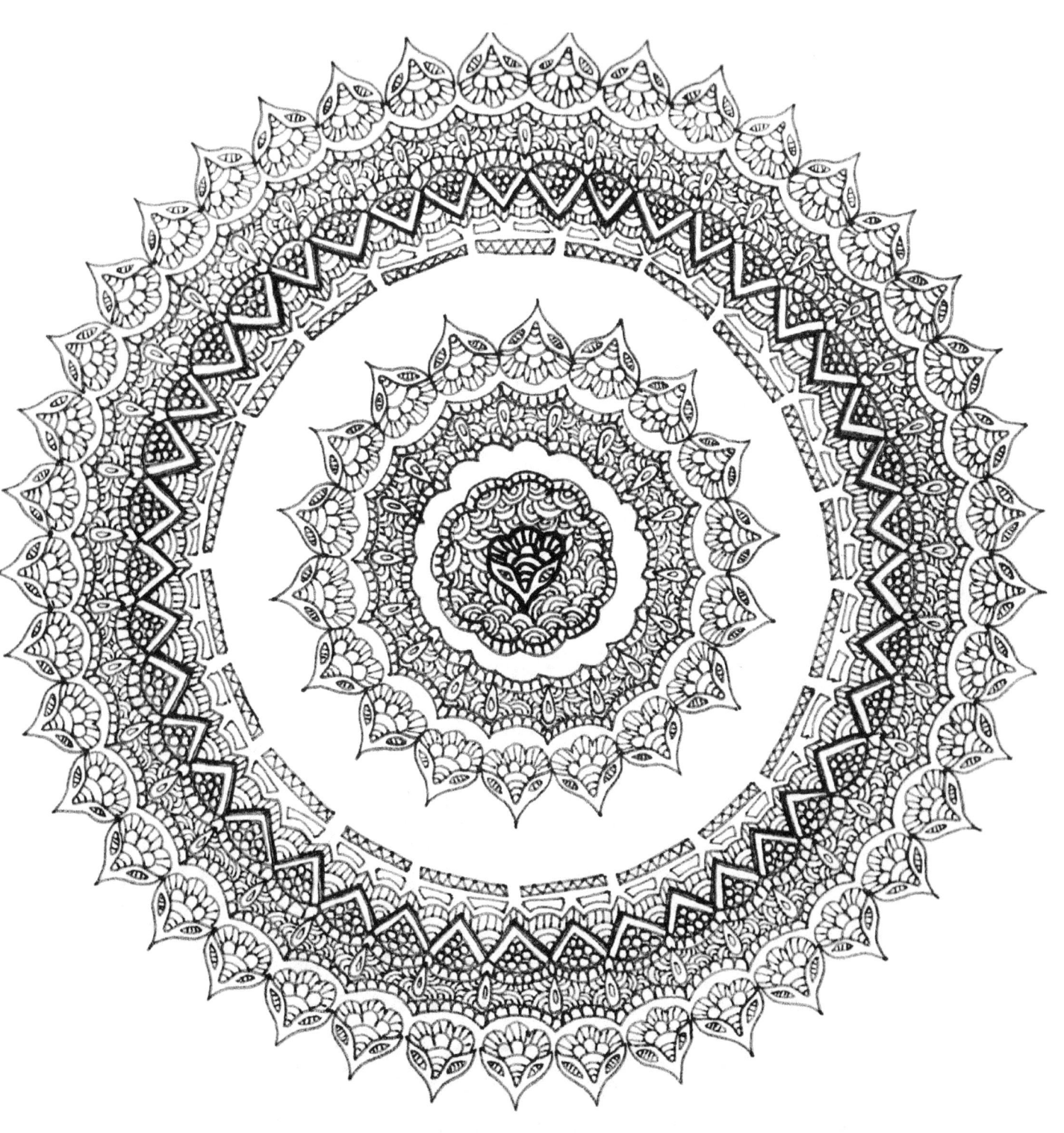

"*Rejoice in hope, be patient in tribulation,*
be constant in prayer."
Romans 12:12

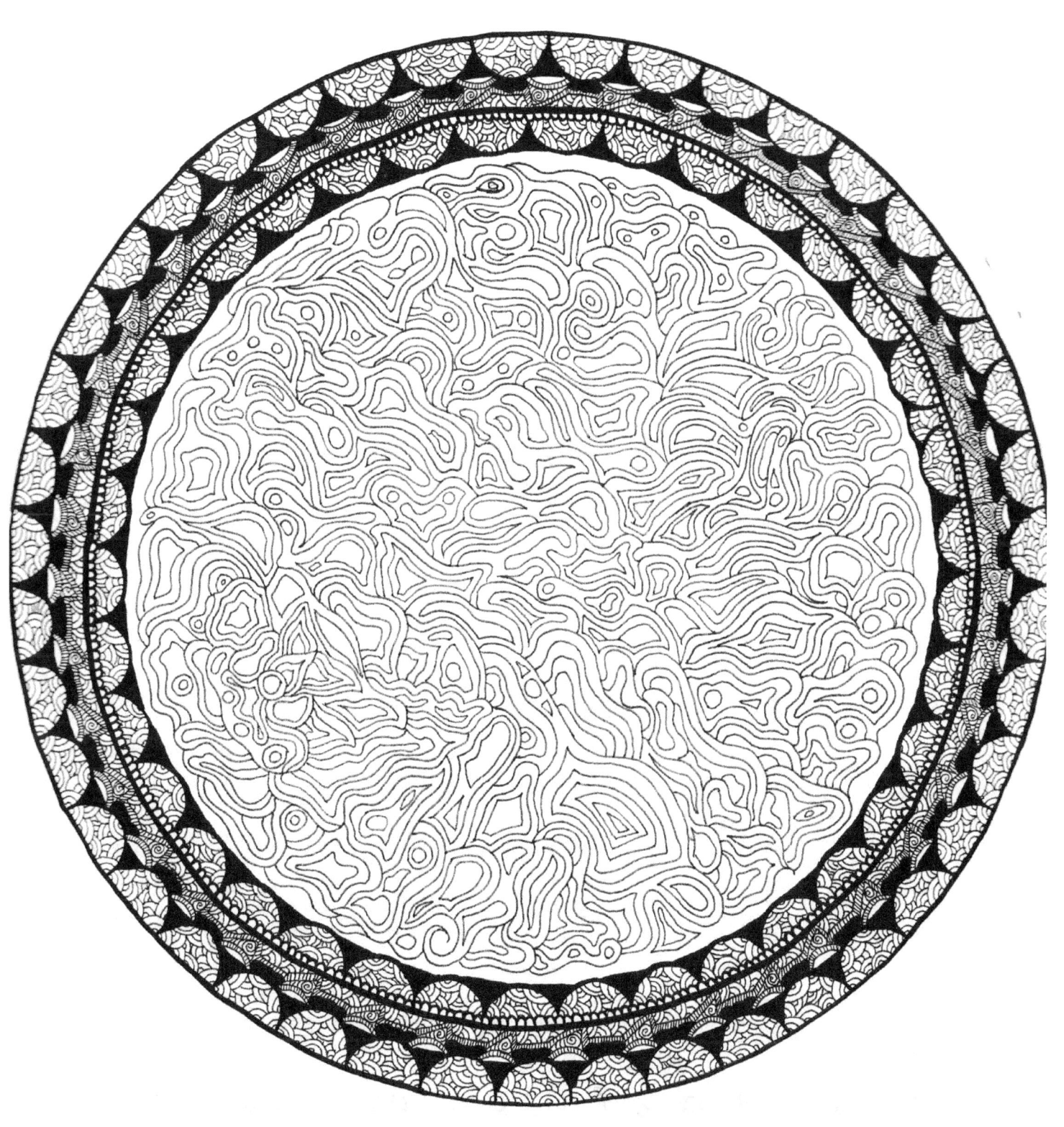

"Jesus answered, 'I am the way and the truth and the life. No one comes to the Father except through me.;"
John 14:6

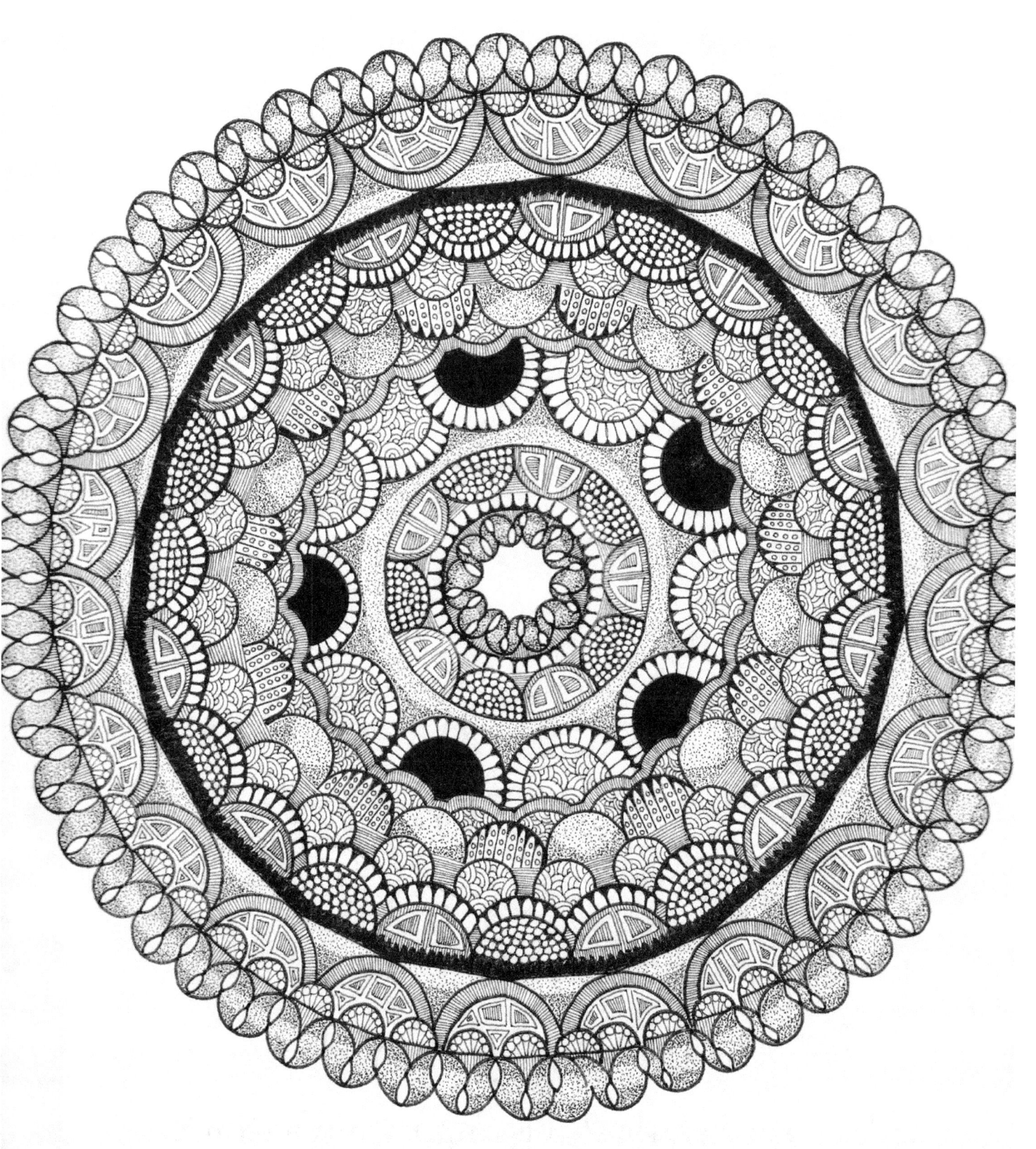

"For nothing will be impossible with God."

Luke 1:37

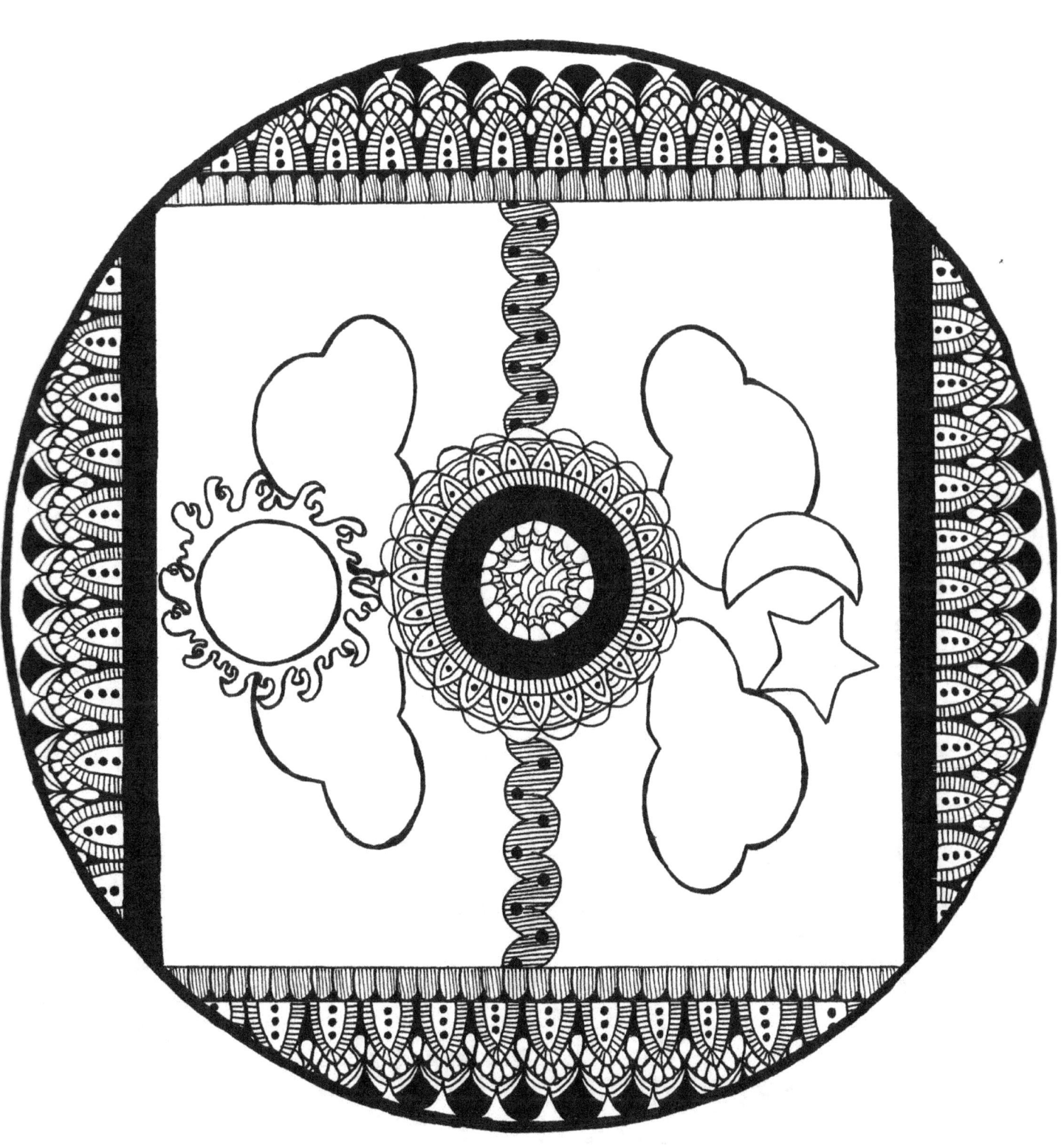

*"The earth is the Lord's, and all it contains,
The world, and those who dwell in it."*
Psalm 24:1

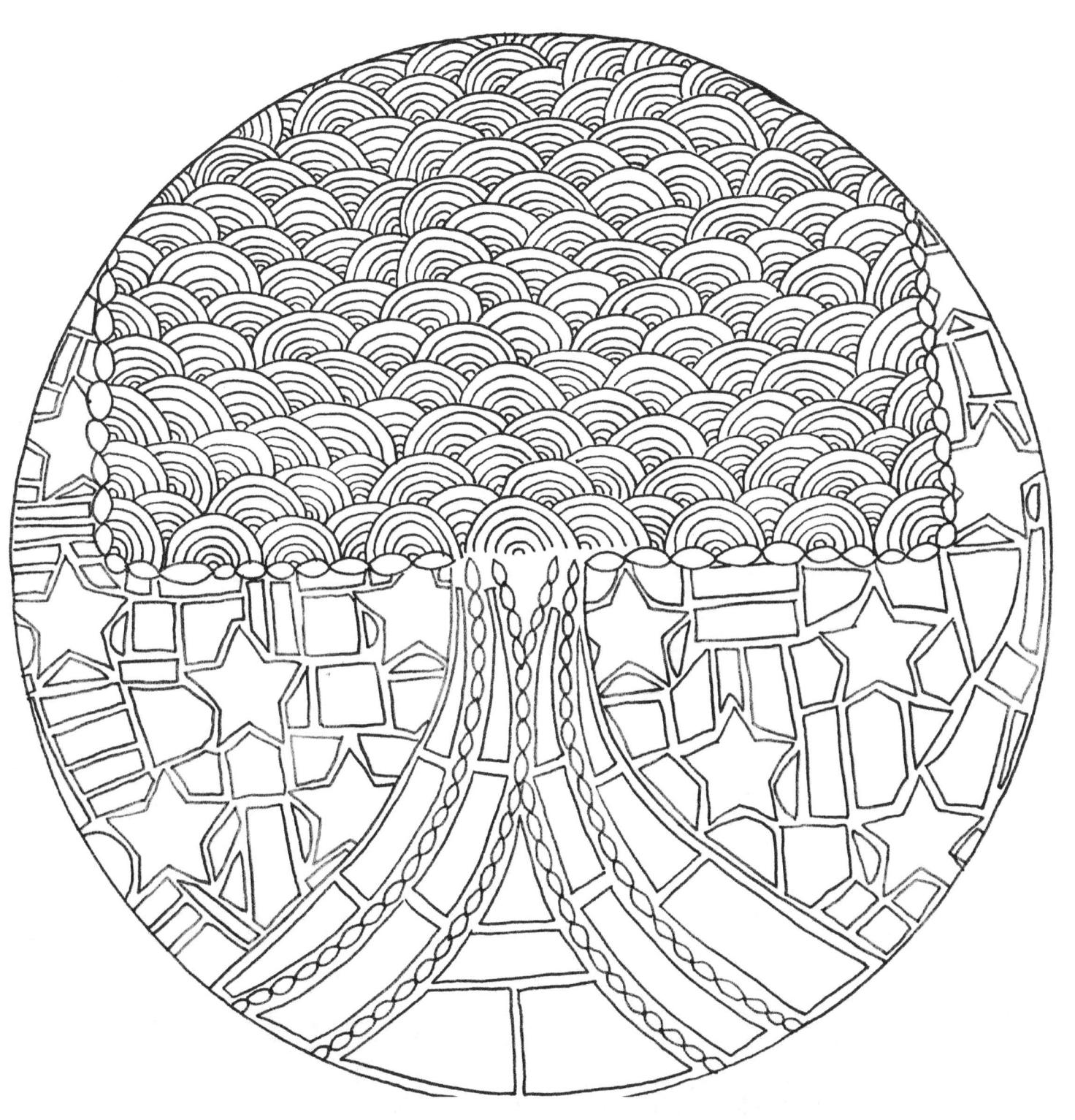

"*Rejoice always; pray without ceasing;
in everything give thanks...*"
1 Thessalonians 5:16-18

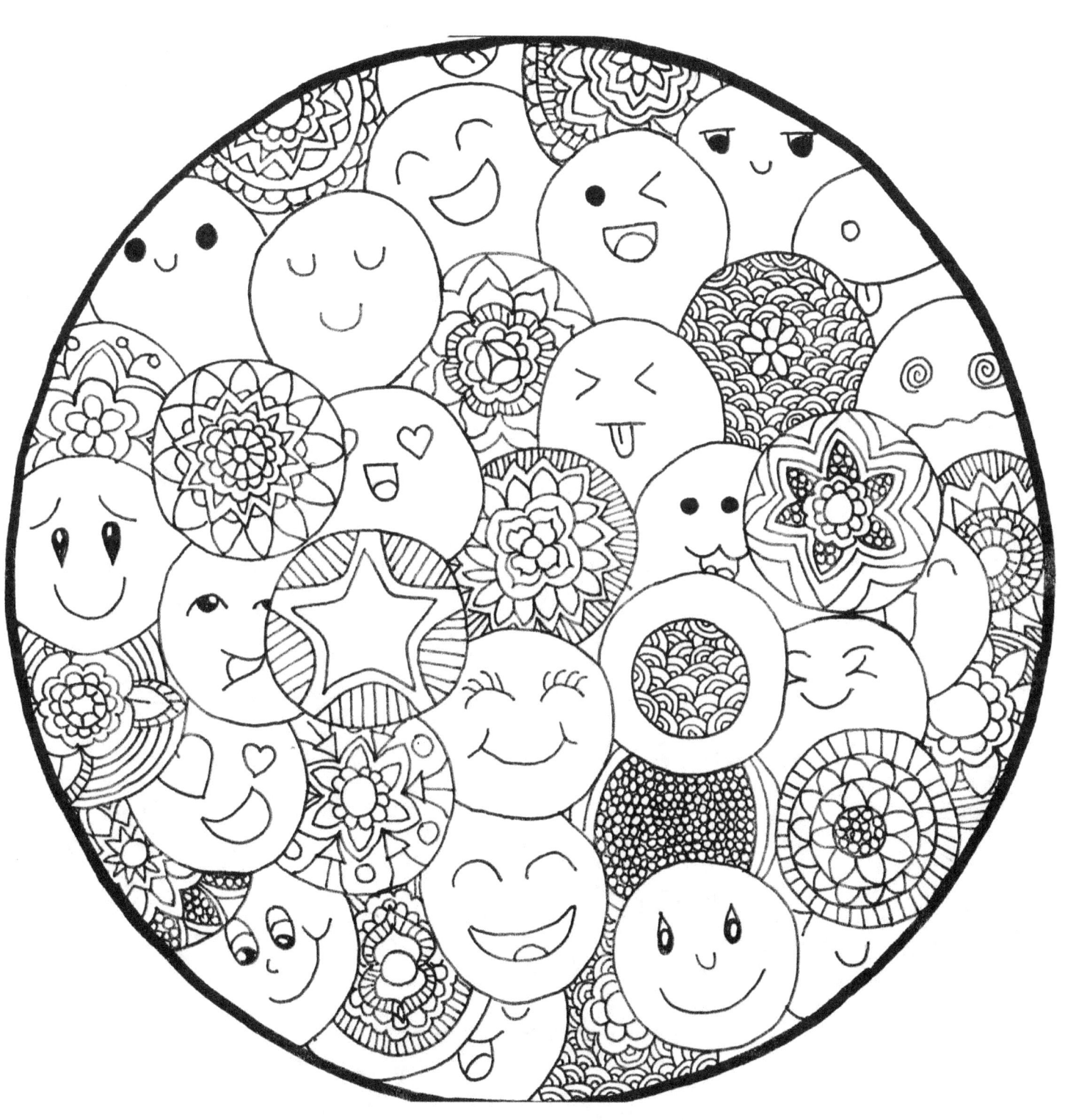

www.ingramcontent.com/pod-product-compliance
Lightning Source LLC
Chambersburg PA
CBHW080914220526
45467CB00024BA/2786